GW00493026

AMBIGUITIES

CHRISTOPHER GEORGIOU

**Nerrigundah
Publishing**

© 2008 Nerrigundah Publishing
19 Coyne Street Fadden ACT 2904
Telephone: 61 262911705
 URL: http://www.maureenburdett.com.au/np/index.htm
Poetry: Christopher Georgiou
Layout: Nerrigundah Publishing

Printed in Australia by Goanna Print Canberra ACT
Cover - 300gsm Sovereign Silk Art
Text - 128gsm Sovereign Silk Art

This book is copyright. Apart from any fair dealing for the
purpose of private study, research, criticism and review, as
permitted under the Copyright Act, no part of this publication
may be produced, stored in or introduced into a retrieval system,
or transmitted, in any form or by any means without the prior
written permission of both the copyright owner of the individual
work and the above publisher of this book.

Editor: Maureen Burdett
Line Drawings: Christopher Georgiou

Cover:
Photograph   The Aegean Island, Telendos.
Photographer   Christopher Georgiou
Design and Artwork   Caroline Ambrus

National Library of Australia Cataloguing-in-Publication entry:
Author   Georgiou, Christopher, 1937-
Title   Ambiguities / Christopher Georgiou
ISBN   978-0-9577375-5-6 (pbk)
Notes   Includes index.
Dewey Number   A821.4

ACKNOWLEDGEMENTS

Previously Published:
Innis Clare.
Heraldry & Geneaology Society
Canberra ACT Australia 2007.

Previously Performed:
I am Patel; Is This Love; Prelude to a Phone Call and *Daddy's Girl.*
Designer/Director: Salvatore Forino
in collaboration with: Marcella Puppini's Forget Me Nots Orchestra
Chelsea Theatre, London UK.

I am indebted to Bobby Pinkerton for her initiative and encouragement and to Maureen Burdett, my Publisher, for her unfailing patience and editorial wisdoms. Thank you.

FOREWORD

Christopher Georgiou is a man who has travelled widely and lived in a variety of cultures. He brings these experiences in a range of forms to this body of work.

Ambiguities is a very diverse collection of poems which moves easily through the full spectrum of human emotions, from the anger and guilt generated by friends helplessly watching death in *John's Room* to the writer's tongue in cheek observation of news presentation in *Breaking News*. The poems are also wide ranging in time from the author's memories of a childhood on the New South Wales south coast in *Laughter on the Lake* to the immediacy of *The Battle for Basra*.

Many of Christopher's poems are characterised by a poignancy that gives them a very powerful edge. This is most evident in the shorter pieces such as *...and die a Greek* and *The Fall*. There is also an honesty in his poetry. He describes life as he sees it and holds nothing back from the reader. His poems exhibit a keen observation of the human condition, but more than this they display his deep sympathy for the less fortunate of his subjects.

The poems follow an easy rhythmic style, which alternates seamlessly between rhyming and free verse formats and their appeal is enhanced by the author's creative use of imagery, exemplified by his "damply nodding daffodils" in the poem *Enchantment*.

This is a collection that is engaging, sometimes confronting, but always accessible by the reader.

David Meyers
4/8/08

Editors Note:
David Meyers is a Poet, Author and Historian who lives and works in Canberra. David's current work is a history of the Limestone Plains on which Canberra is situated.

Contents

Someone Else's Son   9
My Patch   11
Innis Clare   13
Gerry   15
How I Come In Australia   17
Mutual Disability   19
Enchantment   21
Contradictions   22
Anger as Latecomer   23
Kalymnos Isle   26
Living on the Edge   27
Predecessors   29
Death of a Greek Princess   31
John's Room   33
Loss   35
Breaking News   36
Save Our Souls   40
...and Die a Greek   41
Daddy's Girl   45
The Fall   49
The Code   50
The Battle for Basra   52
Thoughts of War   53
Tricky Decisions   55
Lost at Sea   57

Contents

The Battle for Baghdad	60
The Samaritan's Song	61
Paddy's Song	62
Therapy	64
Hillsides	66
Put It on the Tab	68
Children in the Churchyard	72
Gliders	74
Departure	76
For Stanley	81
Chair Bound	83
Tempus Buggerit	84
Prelude to a Phone Call	85
Spring 2004	86
Woman in a Doorway	87
About Bob	89
Morning Call	91
Laughter on the Lake	92
I Am Patel	95
God is Great	100
The Meeting	102
Ambiguities	106
Love Comes	108
To Whom it May Concern	109
St Martin-in-the-Fields	110

cg

6

All that could be carried off
was gone.
No seats. No nave or chancel,
screen or bell.
No place to bow the head and take
the wine soaked bread.

SOMEONE ELSE'S SON

He walked onto their worksite
scruffy, thin and young
and they, hard hatted and hard booted,
watched him come.

Was there, he asked, and standing close
he whiffed a bit, a path
by which he'd reach the motorway
and thumbing, find his way to somewhere
else?
It seemed that anywhere would do.

A chippie, young as he, but tanned,
tattooed and better fed,
emptied the dregs from his mug of tea
and walked away with nothing said.
Somebody else spat sideways
as he climbed on his JCB.

But others, older, more at one
with living's casual cruelty,
saw him as someone else's son
lost in his own fragility.

They gave the directions that he'd asked
and then, when he made to move away,
they gave, unasked, small gifts
they knew would help him through his day.
Filling his jacket with bottled water,
fruit and bread.
No words were said.

He went on into his void
and they, hard hatted and hard booted,
back, perhaps, to theirs.

MY PATCH

I am the man who walks
the central reservation,
selling roses
in this car polluted place,
beneath the roadways' concrete elevation.
This is my patch and some of you,
perhaps the ones who fail to race
the changing lights,
will buy my fading flowers
as you wait.
And take them home to women
at your journey's end,
as gifts of love,
or gestures of inadequate apology.

I walk the central reservation
watching you as you watch me,
locked behind the anonymity
of laminated screens.
Though each pretends
politely not to see.

This is my patch,
this godforsaken place,
I walk it every day
and wait for you to come my way.

Some will offer fumbled coins
through partly opened windows,
in wordless brief exchange
for tired roses, just before
the rhythmic change of engine roar
and then they're gone.
You and others wait
in traffic's endless stream
and waiting, wonder should you buy,
whilst trying not to catch my eye
before the light turns green.

But I can wait.
This is my patch.
I walk this reservation every day.

INNIS CLARE

I left Clare Island on a day
when western mists concealed
its mountain peak
and cold Atlantic spray
flung tears that mingled with my own.
I had no words. I could not speak.

The tears were not for me,
but for the daughters of an Island family
the Flynn girls — Norah, Mary,
Margaret and Winifred.
Those times so hard that
each in turn had left
their white walled cottage home
to find their futures far from
Innis Clare.
Not knowing where.

The girls had gone just as their brothers
Michael, Charles and Patrick;
Luke and John;
and down the years before
so many others
had left their Island home
for distant foreign shores.

The Winters, the Morans and the Gradys;
the O'Malleys and McCabes; they too
had mingled salted tears
with Ireland's ocean spray as
curraghs carried them away,
most never to return.

We are the produce of their dreams,
we nieces, nephews, daughters, sons,
and now these distant decades on
have made our brief return to where
their dreams began on Innis Clare.
And, though we leave,
some deep essential part of us
will stay a longer while,
joined by bloodlines each to each
and ever to this wild and lovely isle.

GERRY

England? Yair I've been to England.
Durin' the war, it was.
Bloody cold and piss-awful beer.
We was in for repairs and some of us
got ashore.
We met some local matelots,
little blokes they were and I could hardly
understand a word they said.
 One especial.
Bigger than the others, and bearded.
"So where you from?" I asked.
 "England," he says.
"Yair, I know you're
a bloody pom," I says,
"but where in England?"
"Liverpool," he says,
which is when he hit me.
It musta took the shore patrol
an hour or more to sort it out.
Meanwhile, him and me,
we took off for another pub.

He drunk a lot more of that piss-awful
beer.
Me? I stuck to proper navy grog.
"We're survivors," he said.
"Too right," I said.
I don't recall his name,
but I heard 'is ship went down off Crete.
England?
Yair, I've been there mate.

HOW I COME IN AUSTRALIA?

I tell you how I come in Australia.
It was on ship. I join him in Piraeus.
I am mechanic.
Not now but then.
We sail for Singapore but one night
BAM! Two times BAM!
with torpedo from Japanese.
So now we are in boats
and ship is going down.
Ti na kanoume? What we do?
Then suddenly
the submarine he's come up
next to us.
Yes right here, like this
and we think
now we are dead
they will kill us.
The Japanese capitano he's up there
and he's shout down
"nearest land is here,"
and he points.
Then they send down big packet
then they start engines again
and they go into dark and disappear.

What you think?
We look in packet and
we find map, small compass, water and
biscuits.
And some brandy.
Yes, brandy.
And soon in one, two days time
we find land.
And then I come here in Australia.
No money, no clothes, no passport.
Many people say they no like Japanese.
Me? I don't know.

You want dessert now, or you wait?

MUTUAL DISABILITY

Profoundly deaf – the words
are printed on the card
I've placed upon your table
amid my spread of plastic Zippos
and torches from Taiwan
that might or might not work
when you have bought and I have gone.

Profoundly deaf.
It tells you so in Greek
and languages I do not know
and, if I knew, I could not speak.
And urges you to buy or,
at the very least, to give
that I can live.

Profoundly deaf.
I cannot read your lips
if you're a Finn or Englishman
or Dane.
Instead I watch your eyes
to see the things I cannot hear you say.
Perhaps disdain,

or disbelief, or simply that
you cannot understand
how things might be
for others in a foreign land
profoundly deaf like me.

You take my card and,
as you read it, raise your eyes
to look at me.
I hope you'll buy,
but still I look away
to keep my dignity.
What does either of us see?
I cannot hear what you won't say.
Here, in this overwhelming silence,
we have a mutual disability.

ENCHANTMENT

Blackbirds rejoicing,
featherwet, in rain
whose every generous spill
make fragrant heathers
bounce again,
lilac against the yellow splash
of damply nodding daffodil.

I watch, entranced,
from dry within,
imprisoned by the rain but still
enchanted by its fill.

I've put aside the Sunday press
with its litany
of mankinds' mindlessness
preferring what I see
through water rippled window pane
the gently healing fall
of Spring's sweet rain.

CONTRADICTIONS

Meeting,
but not meeting.
Talking,
but only in the silence.
More eloquently
than I have ever done.
Touching minds,
glimpsing hearts.
Sharing in some
unfathomable way...

ANGER AS LATECOMER

How long should anger take to come?
In some it flares at once
with incandescence.
In others, or maybe just at other times,
it smoulders darkly.
Long and slow.

Mine has just arrived.
Some seven months beyond the time
I stood amid the crumbling stones
of what was once my father's village
in the foothills of Kyrenia.

What once was Greek is now
the home of Turks
by means of uninvited armed persuasion.
A brooding place and seemingly
devoid of dogs and children.
I saw no school.
A sullen Turk or two regarded me
with watchful eyes.

I climbed the steps of what had been
the village church.

It seemed, deceptively, intact
until I stepped inside
and saw it for the gutted shell it has
become.
All that could be carried off
was gone.
No seats. No nave or chancel,
screen or bell.
No place to bow the head and take
the wine soaked bread.
Where once the cantors would have sung
now broken icons mutely tell
of religious insanity.
I stood in that desecrated, dusty place
and felt only sadness
for the village lost, its people gone.

But now, these many months and miles
beyond,
I've stood awhile and watched
the cold Atlantic fall upon
this English shore.
And feel at last the anger rise in me
as bitter bile.

I should have, oh I should have,
oh I know now what I should have done.
I should have stepped back
out onto that dusty street
and hauled some startled Turk
back into what had been my father's
father's church.
And asked him, in Australian,
and in Greek, just what
and why the fuck had this been done.
He would not have understood and,
even if he had, he might have said
that this was what
my father's people did to his.

My anger is mine.
He will have his own.

KALYMNOS ISLE

On days that are grey
with winter's cold rain
a tumbler of ouzo
will bring again
the sun's healing warmth
over bright glittered seas
and the smiling
brown faces
with their shy courtesies,
and I too will smile
as I raise my glass
southwards to
Kalymnos isle.

LIVING ON THE EDGE

It's calculated that
some twenty million people
now inhabit Oz
and nearly all of us
live clinging to
Australia's edge
and stay in spitting distance
of its seas.

For this vast land does not
extend its welcome much beyond
the Western Plains
where only Aborigines
can understand
its mysteries,
and even they, seduced, destroyed
by all that's worst
in white society
have all but given up.

Their tribes were once
the Guardians of these lands.
But we have locked them out
and thrown away the keys.

And now we twenty millions
invade, relentlessly, the Bushland,
reducing it to blocks
of real estate;
of boutique buildings
and polyurethane designer kitchens
with "Customer Commitment Guarantees".

We mill about in ducted aircon
shopping malls,
trapped by our unsustainability.
Whilst the shattered Bushland weeps
and curlews cry its loss.

PREDECESSORS

We are your predecessors
we Pharaohs, Kings and humbler men
we lived here then,
each in our time
as vividly as you live now
in yours.

Our passions were no less strong
our lusts and laughter filled our years
we built the world to which
you now belong.
We fed it with our blood
we washed it in our tears.

We were as arrogant as you
we thought that what we had
was all that there could ever be
and so we schemed and fought
and, without knowing,
made our marks
on what, for you, is history.
You'll find us in our burial mounds
and in the footprints of our homes,
look for us drowned
among the ribs of sunken ships,

remark upon our polished bones.
Admire, perhaps revere, the things
we've left behind, those artifacts
that you will find.
And, in your turn, leave memories
for others still to come.

DEATH OF A GREEK PRINCESS

She tried to swim the Strait
but drowned.
The legend says
she swam to meet the man
she loved.
Their love prevented
by the protocols
of feuding families.

But still she swam to meet her man.

And this a thousand years
and more
before the Playwright wrote
of Juliet and of the man
she loved.

But this Princess must certainly
have known
the waters here
run fast and deep
and yet she tried
and, trying, died alone.

And ever since that time,
the locals say,
the mountainside retains
in stone
her profiled image.
It can be seen most strikingly at dusk
and yet again at dawn.

And there are fishermen
who say that, still
she swims the strait
in vain
to meet the man she loves.
And swims, and dies.

And swims again.

JOHN'S ROOM

This is a room in which it's hard
to find God's gifts.
John's room.
Nurses plump pillows
and fiddle with pale plastic tubes
as we stand awkwardly by.
Three older men watching
a younger man die.
And John, now Belsen thin,
condemned to
spastic facial tics and
almost inarticulate reply,
watches from a distance
that has grown
a little more
since we were here before.

God's gifts are difficult to find
His mercies don't come easily
to mind.

Framed photos offer images
of John in happy times
and better places
drinking beer with friends,

or posing proudly with a fish
he'd caught at sea
but even then he knew
that his remaining years
were few.

The nurses go
and we resume our flow
of adolescent banter.
We try to fill the space.
But the jokes we make
are made to cover anger
at the cruelty of it all
and the guilt we feel
by knowing we can walk away.

We promise to return
but as we go we see him
turn to face the wall.

God's gifts are difficult to find.
His mercies don't come easily
to mind.
Not here in John's room.

LOSS

Where once love filled
the empty spaces
now there are
only silences between
and I am left
uncomprehendingly
bereft.

BREAKING NEWS

The reader of the morning news
On TV's early breakfast show
shuffles papers,
smiles and nods,
his teeth a tribute
to his orthodontist's skills
and God's,
as he recites the litany
of all the usual ills
of revolutions, football failures
and murders overnight.
And as he speaks
a rolling caption
scrolls the screen
with words that tell
of melting icecaps,
tumbling shares.
All is well,
or possibly
as well as all can be.

Then, as he speaks,
there comes a pause.
He looks away

with finger pressed against his ear
and back again to us
and the rolling, scrolling
caption tells of "Breaking News"
and nothing,
not one single thing,
will ever be the same.

We are, he tells us,
going over to our correspondent
in Washington DC.
And so we do and there he stands,
our Man,
lit garish by the TV lights
and warmly clad
to meet the chill
of winter nights
on Capitol Hill.

His words dispersing puffs
of steaming breath
he tells us of reports
from scientists in observatories
on mountain tops and other
solitary places,

reports that several disturbingly
large chunks of rock,
impelled by cosmic force,
that should have passed us
safely by,
have made an unexpected
shift in course
that causes them to intertwine
their interplanetary orbit
with that of
yours and mine.

He pauses, listens,
looks to us again.
"It seems," he says,
"we're due to meet
in several minutes time."

The barest wobble on our screens
betrays a tremor of
the Camera Operator's hand.
And then, abruptly, we return
to where our Anchor Man
sits, ashen, at his desk.
And "Breaking News"

continues scrolling by
with words informing
that our sky
will fill with tumbling rocks
from outer space
and we should better
find some safer place.

Our reader smiles uncertainly
as though he hopes there must be
some mistake
"It seems," he says, "we've lost our link
with Washington DC.
But we'll take that story up
beyond the break
when we come back."

And that is when
the screens go black.

SAVE OUR SOULS

Everything that ever was
remains.
Every molecule and atom
every grain
each healing, drowning
fall of rain
will stay.
Nothing ever leaves this planet
save our souls.

...AND DIE A GREEK

Some day,
when others have to turn me
in my bed,
I'll think of now.
My memories will be as clear
and my limbs as strong.
And, in my head,
I'll swim again
these warm Aegean seas
and die a Greek.

cg

I heard your nearness
in the resonating sounds
of steel on steel,
in parody of bells that peal
on Sundays in Murmansk.

DADDY'S GIRL

He flicks the ball
to knee to head
and back to toe
and looks to see
if she admires his
— ball control, his versatility.

She looks away.

"Come on sweetheart
where will daddy take us,
where is it we want to go?"
And she, she smiles
her small uncertain smile
and says what he will want
to hear her say.
"To the playground, daddy,"
and waits,
"that's where we'll
go and play."

And mother watches from a window.

"She isn't doing so well,"

the teacher pauses,
delicately choosing words,
"not near as well as others
in her class."
And mother waits.
"She seems unduly..."
the word comes out with care,
"...introspective,"
a *silence hangs between them*
"hardly ever joining in
with other eight year olds."
Through the study window
come the sounds of other
not so introspective eight year olds
at play.
"We felt you ought to know."

"That kid next door?
you hardly ever see her smile.
What's with her anyway?
You talk to her
She doesn't have a thing to say.
Just mooches round

and spends her days off school
alone, or with her dad..."

"Hey little pigeon,
how about we read some stories
together? The way you
like us to."
She sits unmoving,
staring at the screen.
"You'd like that, wouldn't you?"
She nods but doesn't look at him
"You go on up," he says
"pick something that you'd like,
I'll come and see you soon."
His wife picks up the TV Times
and reads the same page yet again.
And, later, goes to bed alone.

"She harms herself," the
mother says,
"in places that it doesn't show
she burns and cuts..." *her voice trails off*
in helpless resignation.

"I don't know why. I don't know
what to say."

But yet, of course, she knows.

"You don't know why," the doctor asks,
but she won't meet his eye,
"there always is a reason."

The mother only looks away.

"These people, sweetheart,
always asking things
that they don't really
need to know.
We're happy, aren't we babe?
Just you and me.
And mum, of course.
She's happy too.
But not like us."
He flicks the ball
from knee to head to toe.
Tap, tapping it away.

And she has nothing.
Not a thing to say.

THE FALL

He fell, and falling,
dropped through space
and far from friends
into disgrace.
Went bad, said some
and others said,
went mad.
And still he fell
beyond the boundaries of grace.
There were none
who shared his pain and
none who cared enough to see
that he was you
— and you are me.

THE CODE

They came for him at night
'though night in jail
is difficult to know
from daylight hours,
beyond the pale
fluorescent glow
and flatly lit routines.
Bang up; Lock down;
Association; Exercise,
and the Scrubbing of Latrines.

In this place there is only time,
and men, and walls.
And time.

So they came for him
while others looked
the other way.
And no one on that landing
would see or say
what they had heard
above the increased volume
of tobacco bartered iPods
and illicit hardcore DVD.

There was something to be taught
and something learned
and they, the Teachers,
taught him wordlessly
but well the lesson he had earned
that night
beyond the sanctuary of his cell.
They delivered it
with fists and feet
and a sly cold blade.
And he had nowhere to retreat.

In all the time
that would remain
to him inside,
down the wasting,
achingly corrosive years,
he would not again transgress
that harsh inviolable Code.

In this place there is only time,
and men, and walls.
And time.

And time.

THE BATTLE FOR BASRA

It was one of several rounds
of missiles fired.
Each said to cost
about a hundred thousand pounds
and much admired
by students of artillery.

Once launched it flew
and struck a conscript who,
had he been spared,
could not in all his life
have earned so great a sum
as that expended
by that awesome gun.

THOUGHTS OF WAR

How would it be
to hurl myself
into that final, bloody
madness.
Deafened by the thunder
of my own heartbeat.
Heedless of the guns,
determined not to stoop
or swerve.
Intent on death.
How would it be?

How would it be
in another, darker, region
of my heart
beyond societies' civilities.
Where politics and creeds
no longer can pretend
to play a part.
All loves forgotten.
No further infidelities
of mind or soul.
No more pretence,

of loyalties to earthly things.
No further thought
beyond the certainty
that lies ahead,
that dreadful thing
that man does best,
the clear and awful
honesty
— of War.

TRICKY DECISIONS — Going up the Line France 1915

"Good grief," the Colonel said.
"Can that be the time. The fellows
should really be out of their bed
and ready to go up the line."

"But Sir," said the Adjutant, looking
perturbed,
"the fellows won't like it a bit.
This is the day that they usually stay
undisturbed and asleep
in their pit."

"Hmn," said the Colonel, "I see what you mean.
A tricky decision I fear.
Let's see if the Hun
is manning his guns
if not we'll retire to the rear."

"Very well," said the Adj
looking over the edge
to see what the foe
was about...

...when a shattering crack
sent him staggering back
with a hole in his head
and a shout.

And the Colonel remarked,
as he watched him fall,
"Gad, we'd best get 'em up
after all."

— *with apologies to Siegfried Sassoon*

LOST AT SEA
The Russian submarine *Kursk* August 2000

Well, I waited
knowing you would come.
I heard your nearness
in the resonating sounds
of steel on steel,
in parody of bells that peal
on Sundays in Murmansk.

And if my brothers
in the darkness heard, they kept their silence.
Holding in each precious breath.
Delaying death.

And still I waited.
Dreaming of the things I'd do
when rescue comes.
Of summer suns
on Russia's sweet and lovely land
I once enjoyed so carelessly.
Of sisters once again to greet
and women still to meet.

I knew you'd come.

The Navy always saves its own
for we are family.

I knew you'd come.

I knew that we'd be part of
some great rescue scheme
involving skills too difficult
to understand for sailors such as me.
A scheme inspired by admirals and officers
and others of the sea.
A plan to bring us marching home
with pride through Naval towns
to gifts of flowers and pretty girls
and commendations all around.

I knew you'd come.

I've listened to the last and laboured breath
of brothers in the throes of death,
and in the darkness waited still
for you or God to fill

our broken boat with life
and bring us up to blessed light.
The rescue sounds are long since gone
and neither you nor God will come.

But I am waiting still.

THE BATTLE FOR BAGHDAD

Well that's another war won
by us, the righteous
and by the grace of God,
ours of course, not theirs.
We surely are the Chosen Ones.
From medieval times
we've given them to know
what's what.
We Christian types,
we sons of God.
We've invented better missiles,
faster planes and bigger bombs
not to mention chicken burgers,
crisps and Coke.
We know the score.

THE SAMARITAN'S SONG

Are you listening, God?
Do you hear what we hear
down the 'phone lines
in the dark hours?
Do you hear them?
Lost in the night's
anonymity
calling from the darkest reaches
of their souls.
Are you there?
As we are here.
Hearing their despair
listening to their fears
helpless
in our inability
to lift away their pain
tonight. Or any night.
They'll call again.
Tomorrow,
and again.
Will you be there?

PADDY'S SONG
Lt. P. I. McDowell RN ML137 D Day 1944

Many friends are gathered
in the garden
this warm June afternoon.
One man stands and,
in a voice once strong
but echoing now
his more than eighty years,
he sings to us
old Irish songs.
And we stand rapt.

Few listening know,
that, in another June
more than sixty years before,
this then young man,
with others like him,
sailed to war.

They sailed in fragile
wood hulled ships designed
to sweep the shallows clear
of enemy explosive
so ship-borne armies

in their wake
could storm the waiting shore.
History tells the outcome
of that day and the days
that followed.
But it's we, here in this
sunlit garden,
who are witness to the fact
that this good man
survived his war
and all these decades on
can stand and bless us
with his song.
And we are in his debt
once more.

THERAPY

How do we do this doc?
D'you mind that I call you that?
I mean I know you're not a doctor
but it's just that it might help me
justify my coming here.
And I'm only here
because a friend suggests
it could be good for me.

You don't say much do you doc?

Well okay, if this was a cartoon
I'd be reclining on your couch
and you 'd be writing enthusiastically
the things I tell you.
But you don't have a couch
and I don't think I have
that much to say.
Or maybe we should wait and see.

So where do we begin?
Suppose I start by telling you
that, without exception, every man
I've loved
has done his best

to disintegrate my life.
When he's not trying to own me.
I've heard a lot of women say the same
about their men.
Am I some kind of willing victim
d'you think?
I should have learned by now
I know, but even so, it would be good
if I could make a life that isn't complicated
by the things I am.

I'm really tired doc. Almost too tired
to want to live.
This isn't how it ought to be.
Maybe it goes right back to when
my father, in his disappointment,
thought he ought to make
a better man of me.

A better man.
His problem you might say.
And maybe doc, that's really where
we should begin today.

HILLSIDES

"So," he says "here we are.
The two of us.
On our respective hillsides."
He pauses, "indulge me for
suggesting that there is
an 'us'."
She, of course, says nothing.
"Anyway," he blunders
resolutely on, "as I was
saying, you sitting on
your hillside,
and me on mine,
with nothing but these
miles and miles between.
So let me see if I can
look at this, perhaps,
dispassionately."
She only smiles a little – what's
the word? – indulgently.
"How can it be?" he asks,
"that we who have not met,

and know a hundred reasons
that is how it has to be,"
she raises an eyebrow
"have joined in this..." he hesitates
then plunges on "have joined in
this quite beautiful embrace.
How can it be?"
And then she smiles and with
her woman's hard won wisdom says,
"You talk too much,
enjoy."

PUT IT ON THE TAB

"Through a Glass Darkly"
Saint Paul wasn't it?
Well of course it was,
I know that.
But he wasn't seeing things
as I'm seeing them now,
through the bottom of this glass.

His "darkly" is not mine.
In my case, and in my glass,
there are amber lights.
It isn't dark. Instead I'm seeing
reflections of the quite expensive
single malt contained within.
Did you hear that "contained within"?
I'm not, as yet, reduced to drinking
cheaper scotch you know
and there's still some time to go
before I condescend to gin.

Laugh if you will. See it as a joke.
Or more exactly think of me
as a joke, if you must.
But, by the way, I don't.
See myself as a joke that is.

So go to hell if that's what you think.
I'll ask the barkeep for another.
Join me. We'll put 'em on my tab.

So let's get back to Paul.
Saint Paul. Now I know that when
he was talking of "glasses darkly"
it was all to do with the
loss of childhood innocence,
and taking on the all obscuring cloak
of adulthood.
Something along those lines.

Yes, well I could talk to you
about all that.
Better than Saint Paul.
I could tell you -
of marriages and mortgages
and kids whose innocence
I've yet to find.
Not even mine.

Perhaps especially not mine.
And if you want a further list,
well there are straying wives,

and selfish lovers
and bank managers and
Tax collectors,
wasn't one of those a friend of Christ?
Well I can't think of one
who'd ever be a friend of mine.
And lawyers. God protect us from
the lawyers.

Hey, barkeep, we'll have another,
and put it on the tab.

So, back to Paul. Saint Paul.
Now there's a man so totally
enthused by all he'd heard of Christ,
well he'd only heard of him as Jesus then,
but anyway the things he'd heard had fired
him up and sent him off
on journeys that would take him
to places we would only go
with Thomas Cook or Sunset Holidays
or whatever other crap we find
on which to waste our money.

But this was not for him. Not old Paul.
Saint Paul. He did it all the hard way,

walking endless dusty tracks
and hiding, wisely, from the local Law.
He was, as our Motivational Advisors
call it now, a Man on a Mission.
A bringer of Good News to Greeks
and others all around the eastern Med.

Well I don't see too much
Good News right now, do you?
That doesn't mean I haven't tried
but too many other things
are getting in the way.
What you might laughingly call life.

And kids are starving in the Congo
or wherever. What am I supposed
to do about all that? Or you?
And I am at the arse end of my 'radiant' career.
And I don't like people feeling sorry
for themselves.
There are few things worse than
whingeing drinkers. What?
What's so bloody funny?
Yeah, you're right.
We'll have another.

I'll put it on the tab.

CHILDREN IN THE CHURCHYARD

There are children in the churchyard
warmly clad this winter day
in coloured scarves and woolly hats
they fill the air with childish chat
and flit as bright as summer birds
between the cloistered trees.

Despite November's numbing cold
they're happy to be here
beyond enclosing classroom walls
but, even so, they pause when told
and stand quite still,
obedient to their teachers' calls.

The teachers tell of history
and of queens and kings forever dead,
but history is also made of
humbler folk who, in their childhoods'
lightest days, ran laughing through
this ancient churchyard's
flagstoned ways.
Just as these children do.

And it might be wishful thinking
that I fancy I can see,
standing silent in the shadow
of the ever watchful trees,
the souls of those whose bones
lie buried under weathered stones
and smiling as they see
these children fill our world anew
with promised continuity.

GLIDERS

I know you.
I've watched you
slipping effortlessly by
above my garden
and unaware of me
as you defy
the mathematics of earth's gravity
and float upon the air.

I know you.
I've seen the numbers on your
fuselage and wing,
whilst in the trees
the blackbirds sing
of aerial superiority.

I've framed you in binoculars
in vain attempt to see your face.
I am here and you
are using space
to gambol in a third dimension
that is available to you
but not to me.

I've watched you tumble through the sky
in seeming loss of equilibrium
and then, as though you've only just
discovered how to fly,
recover dignity and space
and climb away from terra firma's
dangerous embrace.
I see you and I envy your escape.

DEPARTURE

They took him down this morning
walking out of step
along the corridors
away from where he'd spent
his final days of these
eleven years.
His guardians, as institutionalised
as he, escorting him attentively
as if he might still seek
to flee their practiced custody
before they reached the door
through which he might
return to life.

They gave him to the bureaucratic care
of careless clerks
whose shoulder boards suggested
the authority to keep him there,
if that was what they thought
was what they ought to do.

He'd stayed awake all night
and now he waited
with the resignation

of a skybound traveller
waiting to be processed
through Departures
to his flight.

They took their time
in filling out laboriously
pointless forms
with plastic ballpoint pens.
Reluctantly returning his
pathetic few possessions,
the forgotten things
he'd brought with him
those years before.
But he at last would now walk free
and they would still be there.

Beyond the barbed wire and the gate
Africa and life await.

cg

"Excellent," you said, with all your
two and a half years of certainty.
And I, at sixty nine, could do no better
but agree.
"Excellent."

FOR STANLEY

We had the loveliest time today,
you and I.
Grandson and Grandfather.
We visited horses
or, more precisely, they visited us.
You stood on the five barred gate
and they came, with ears pricked,
offering in greeting
their warm muzzles
for us to touch.
You loved it, balanced there,
wobbling a little on that gate.
Across the field a digger dug
into the soil.
"A hole," you said with glee.
"It's digging a hole,"
and so it was.
It squeaked and rattled
and, after a while, the digger driver
stepped down to do something
fairly important.
We couldn't see from
where we were,
but it seemed quite interesting.
You laughed, as only

a two and a half year old can do.
And so did I.
We watched another digger,
digging as they do
and as we did, a horse came trotting by
pulling a small cart and driver
— a gypsy perhaps.
We watched together,
you and I, and waved,
and he waved too.
We found a small set of sturdy steps
along the farm approach and I
stood by and watched you climb
uncertainly, and wobble yet again
on reaching the top. And jump.
"Excellent," you said, with all your
two and a half years of certainty.
And I, at sixty nine, could do no better
but agree.
"Excellent."

CHAIRBOUND

I watched him
lolling sideways in his chair,
pushed by his carer through
the glory of a golden day
in spring
when everything and everyone
seemed strong and bright
but him.

I wondered who he was,
and what uncaring fate
brings him, and, maybe, each of us
in time
to this unholy state.

Seeing him like so
I saw what might perhaps be me.
But, on its heels,
there came another thought
 "How weak," it said, "how bleak it is
to think like that,
how patronising can you be
that he, chair bound, may yet
have strengths
that you have still to see?"

TEMPUS BUGGERIT

I shave
and scan my image
in the misted glass
in search of me.
But I'm not there.
The falling features,
thinning hair
belong to someone else.

I wear this horseshoe ring
I bought when I was
almost seventeen.
I know that it's the same
its molecules remain.

But what became of me?

PRELUDE TO A PHONE CALL

Is this some kind of crossing
of a line
to want to hear her voice
and give her mine?
Are we two now to know
all that there is
that we should know?
Yet, even so,
we've still to touch.
Or is that too a step
too much?
And do these liberties
that we might take
come far too soon,
or far too late?

SPRING 2004

The day is slipping sideways
with the setting sun.
I sit enchanted,
listening to the sounds
of roosting birds.
"Ah," say the environmentalists,
the ones who know,
"this is nothing like it was.
All is in decline."
I hear it differently.
The woods reverberate with
echoing call of blackbird and cooing
collared doves.
If this is decline,
then decline is what I'll take
and die myself, in glorious decline,
sung to death by songbirds
whose lovely rhyme
will outlast the environmentalists
and me.

WOMAN IN A DOORWAY

I really have to write this for you
even though I know
I'll never know you.
We have not met,
and will not meet.
And yet, I know your face
and most of all your eyes.
Though in that brief, brief moment
that I saw you
you did not see me.
                `

You, waiting at the entrance
to the village store,
a woman lost.
Your gaze unwaveringly
fixed upon the man inside.
Your man, who'd brought you here
and without whom you'd never find
your way again.

A woman lost
and uttering the small
distressful sounds

as does a child whose parent
momentarily moves from sight.
You in the autumn of your adult years
have fallen back to share
the infant's plight.
Its sense of loss is yours.

Whatever steals our minds
is so much crueler
than the cancers that erode
our bodies' cells.
They can be fought
but, when the mind is robbed,
all its memories gone,
what happens to our souls?

I touched your shoulder
as I passed you in that doorway
and, very fleetingly,
the person you once were
responded with your eyes,
was here once more.
And then, as quick,
was lost again.

ABOUT BOB

He waits for death.
The start, perhaps,
of endless night.
Confidence that came
with youth,
all the certainties
of faith,
desert him now.
There's little sense
in all that went before.
Long years
of fated meetings,
urgent couplings,
jobs begun, journeys started,
destinations never reached.
Unimportant now.
Except for this; the final one.

His friends,
urgent in their need
to ease his dying,
caress his brow
and grope for words
they hope will help him go.

They cannot know,
and he cannot tell them,
what he himself has still to know.

He waits.
Hearing his heartbeat,
feeling it pulsing at his
wasted throat.
Erratic as the flutter
of garden birds.

MORNING CALL

It's four a.m. or so.
I hear, impossibly,
the song of birds
that do not fly
these English skies.
The rolling call of currawong,
the oriole,
and fluting butcher bird.
They don't belong.

There is no Bushland here,
no Ghost Gum eucalypt
or Cabbage Tree nor Moreton Bay.
My hearing does me wrong.

But even so I know I hear them
welcoming my day.

LAUGHTER ON THE LAKE
Lake Illawarra NSW Australia

Here beside the lake
the early winter sun
still offers blessing
with its warmth
and bathes the distant ranges
in a clear and radiant light.

Those are the hills and ranges
of vanished boyhood
and this lake, then as now,
a playground for us all
who lived along its shore.

Here we sailed and fished
and swam
and clumsily began
to grapple with the mysteries
of adolescent life and love.

But I've been out of place
too long.
Until today.

And now I sit and feel
the breeze upon my skin
and listen to it rattling
through the dry and dusty trees
and hear the cawing of the crows.

Sat upon the jetty's weathered rails
the cormorants stretch out
their wings in supplication
to the warming sun
and pelicans take
majesterial flight.

All is as it's always been
here on the lake
and I've been out of place
too long. Until today.

Across the quiet waters
come the sounds of men
whose afternoon is being spent
contentedly afloat
and fishing.
From time to time their outboard

throbs a little, dies and splutters
back to life again.
But there is no urgency for them
and I am glad
to hear their laughter
drifting back
across the lake.

It blesses me
and I am
back in place again.

I AM PATEL

I beg your pardon but
I've seen you in my shop
before.
You buy your paper here
I know, and we have sometimes
passed the time of day
and so I feel
I'd like to introduce myself.
I am Patel.
You'll recognise the name
above my door.

Patel. A name as common
in my culture as Wilkinson
or Smith in yours. Patel.
It tells you that
we're farmers or,
more exactly that
that is what our forebears were.
Men of the soil.
But now, and here, you find us
selling groceries and lotteries,

and-on-the-top-shelf
out-of-reach-to-children
magazines.
Or driving cabs.

We're also, I can say with pride,
we're also gynaecologists and lawyers
and Civil, oh so civil, Engineers.
But that is less how people here,
perhaps not you yourself,
perceive us.
In fact most people here
refer to us as "Pakis"
or as "Asians"
and often worse.
It is as though we think of you
and Irishmen and Portuguese
and Danes as simply being
all the same.
Your languages and culture becoming
unimportant.
I'd guess you'd not be
very much impressed.
And so I'd like to tell you that

my people come originally from
India. And, more exactly, that we are
Gujeratis, as proud a people as any
here on earth can be.
Our lands so fertile they provide
the population with two crops
in every year.
And that makes Gujarat the envy of
our brothers in so many regions
where the soil, so poor,
is little more than dust.
It might be said we're truly blessed.

So why then do you find us here?
The story of each immigrant is never,
ever, quite so clear.
My family had settled in Uganda
long ago
when the going there
was good
and there were livings to be made
and there we flourished.
My older brothers
were sent to University.

One went on to law
and so became a Barrister
in Canada,
the other into pharmacy.
But there was never quite enough
to afford the same for me.

But all of that was doomed,
as one might say,
when racism and thuggery
deprived us of our livelihoods
and liberties
and we, like Jews before us,
were scattered to the winds.
So that is how
my family came here.
And this is how you find us.

My children are at University
and doing well.
And I am here to sell your
Daily Telegraphs and cans of soup
and multi-packs of beer.
To most I am the "Paki"

at the corner store.
But you, at least, you now
know more.

I am Gujerati
and my name is Jag Patel.

GOD IS GREAT

Freshly showered
he stands before the mirror
and wipes the glass
to see himself the better.
This is his day.
Outside the early sun
that now shines warm and bright
has sent away
the heavy humid night.
This is his day.

He thinks again
of those he loves
and knows he loves
them now with
even more intensity
than at any time before.
But this is not their day.

And so he cleans his teeth
and runs the tap
to clear the sink,
and checks once more

the Velcro strap
that takes the weight
of what he wears
beneath his shirt,
and knows the moment
when the 'phone must ring.
Then when it does,
he hears the warm
familiar voice that seems
to sing the words
he needs to hear.

"Allah" the caller says,
"Allah hu akhbar."

And he returns the ancient
God sent words,
and knows his day,
and that of unknown others
unaware,
must now begin.

THE MEETING

I flew Premium Economy
to Oz.
And then I drove to Canberra
and on the way
I killed a kangaroo.

It's worth the extra cost,
you know,
the seats you get are wider
than the ones that go
much further back
towards the tail.
Not only that, you get a glass
of bubbly
when you come on board.

But the roo came out of nowhere
as I drove.

The food is really not that bad
considering you're eating it
at thirty thousand feet and more,
and some of the Australian wines

are really rather good.
So, somewhere over Kakadu,
and when I'd watched a feature film,
I settled down to sleep.
Below, Australia waited in the dark.
I couldn't know, of course, that
at a time and place down there
a kangaroo and I
would have a date to keep.

I began the drive from Sydney
just before the sun was up
and I tuned the radio along the way.
Whilst, perhaps, the kangaroo was licking
at the early morning dew
I was listening to Bach and
looking forward to my day.

Apart from some gigantic trucks
the traffic on the Hume was sparse
and this new day
betrayed the endless pasture
brown with drought struck grass.

It was somewhere just beyond a sign
to Hanging Rock,
when Bach had changed to Verdi,
that our destinies,
the kangaroo's and mine,
would interlock
and fatally entwine,
and one of us would die.

We met at something over
eighty miles an hour.
There was no time to swerve or slow
and so it was the 'roo would have to go.
The car and I, we staggered on,
one shocked, the other battered
by the blow.
I didn't see what happened to the 'roo
but he would certainly have not survived.

In another, grander scheme of things,
if it was me that wandered
lost and helpless through the bush,
it might be me that died.
But here it was the 'roo

was out of place, not I.
Or is that really true?

The rental people were really very kind
expressing more concern for me
than for the broken car I left behind.

I travelled on,
but something intricate had changed
and something beautiful was gone.

AMBIGUITIES

I've seen him before.
Increasingly it seems.
Or maybe it's that I've become
a little more
aware of him in recent times.
He seems to know me
and, in some way,
I feel that I should know him.
I think he thinks I should.
An aging figure, slightly stooped
with a distinctive walk
that is unnervingly familiar.

Once we passed each other
close enough that I could see
the breeze disturb his thinning hair.
He looked at me. His eyes that
faded gray that old men have.
He caught my look
and gave a rueful smile
that seemed to say,
"We've shared this road
a long, long while

and though there may still be
some way to go,
it has its end.
And so do we."

LOVE COMES

Love comes unexpected,
uninvited,
like an ambush in the night.
Fight it, flee it
or embrace it.
Capture or be captivated,
open out your soul to light.

TO WHOM IT MAY CONCERN

Is this what love is?
Oh yes, I think it is.
I can feel the texture
of your skin,
and see the flush of
rosy flesh between
the junction of your neck
and shoulder.
And hear your voice.
and feel your nipple
rise to meet
my touch.
Oh yes.

But love is this
it's all of this and more
a meeting of our souls
a yearning to become
each others'
other part.
Components of the whole,
companions of
the heart.

ST MARTIN-IN-THE-FIELDS

He took the wafered bread
and ate, and wept
the tears he'd kept
too long inside.
And felt the hand upon his head
and heard
the gentle ancient words
"This is my body, this is my blood."
He took the wine
and drank and wept,
knowing,
but not understanding,
why.

cg

Christopher Georgiou working on the manuscript
for Ambiguities. Canberra Australia 2008.

About the Author

Of Greek Cypriot and Irish parents, Christopher Georgiou spent the years from early childhood to young manhood in New South Wales; in Sydney and the Illawarra. He then went to England for what grew from an intended year to permanent residence. He is married with two sons and a grandson. Now 71, he also retains close links with family and friends in Australia, returning whenever possible. His work in the documentary film industry has taken him to many countries filming civil and oil engineering projects; something he has found satisfying and challenging. Christopher began writing as a schoolboy in Wollongong NSW and has continued, intermittently, to write poetry and short stories over the years. This continued interest and body of writing has culminated in *Ambiguities*.

First Line Index

	Page
Are you listening, God?	61
Blackbirds rejoicing	21
England? Yair I've been to England	15
Everything that ever was	40
Freshly showered	100
Good grief the Colonel said	55
He fell, and falling	49
He flicks the ball	45
He took the wafered bread	110
He waits for death	89
He walked onto their worksite	9
Here beside the lake	92
How do we do this Doc?	64
How long should anger take to come?	23
How would it be	53
I am the man who walks	11
I beg your pardon but	95
I flew Premium Economy	102
I know you	74
I left Clare Island on a day	13
I really have to write this for you	87
I shave	84
I tell you how I come in Australia	17
I watched him	83
I've seen him before	106

First Line Index

	Page
Is this some kind of crossing	85
Is this what love is?	109
It was one of several rounds	52
It's calculated that	27
It's four a.m. or so	91
Love comes unexpected	108
Many friends are gathered	62
Meeting	22
On days that are grey	26
Profoundly deaf – the words	19
She tried to swim the Strait	31
So, he says, here we are	66
Some day	41
The day is slipping sideways	86
The reader of the morning news	36
There are children in the churchyard	72
They came for him at night	50
They took him down this morning	76
This is a room in which it's hard	33
Through a Glass Darkly	68
We are your predecessors	29
We had the loveliest time today	81
Well that's another war won	60
Well, I waited	57
Where once love filled	35

GOANNA PRINT

**Nerrigundah
Publishing**

116